POETIC HOLD-UP

POETIC HOLD-UP

NINA CABANAU

RESOURCE *Publications* · Eugene, Oregon

POETIC HOLD-UP

Resource Publications
An Imprint of Wipf and Stock Publishers
199 W. 8th Ave., Suite 3
Eugene, OR 97401

www.wipfandstock.com

PAPERBACK ISBN: 978-1-6667-3373-0
HARDCOVER ISBN: 978-1-6667-2865-1
EBOOK ISBN: 978-1-6667-2866-8

11/02/21

My sincere thanks go to Miami poet Clark Bonilla and to his amazing editing and insightful work on this collection.

My thanks also goes to my translator friend Thomas Ruiz who reviewed the final manuscript and to my best reader—my father Jean-Claude Cabanau.

Contents

4 | Multilingual poetry

5 | A game of love. . .

6 | History's withered roses

1

About poetry

Quando la poesia avrà rinunciato alla sua vita / When poetry will have given up its life (Italian and English)

Quando la poesia sarà estinta

(When poetry will have disappeared),

I will go and cross the black continent of prose,

And the night will rain remorse on me.

I will find your silhouette standing on my inkwell,

I will embrace the perfumes of the roses gone.

Quando la poesia avrà vissuto

(When poetry will have lived),

I will make up my eyes with Indian ink,

I will cut the paper of the night.

To write my dreams in the light of the stars,

I will go and lie down on the rocks scattered in the winds.

Quando la poesia si sarà taciuta

(When poetry will be silent),

I'll grab the naked arm of prose,

I will fight a duel with the shadow of a poem.

The red night will fall in ashes,

My lyre will find death in its bed of black stars.

Quando la poesia s'avrà messo al bando

(When poetry will be banished),

I will go and find the Devil, he shall see my tears,

I will howl the end of love.

And in a castle of forgotten verses,
I'll turn myself into paper.

Quando la poesia avrà rinunciato alla sua vita,
(When poetry will have given up its life),
So that prose comes out of oblivion,
I will bow down before the eternal snow in fire,
I will pursue the radiance of your smile everywhere,
I will let a passionate music spring from the cities.

Poetic Hold-Up

I bought AK47s, 7.62mm rounds.
I'm gonna hold up poetry tonight,
Hold up the words and rhymes,
And the night smothers me with its maternal advice.

I'm putting on a white mask, a black shirt.
I'm gonna hold up poetry tonight,
I'm going down the boulevard full beams on.
The stars are shooting at me.

My hands are clenched on the neck of the night.
I bought a van on the black market.
I'm gonna rob the poetry tonight,
And the moon has an anonymous beauty.

I fired three shots at the beauty of the evening.
I have shot poetry; I am leaving.
Paris gave me its light while trembling,
And the night cried silver tears.

Bright star

Bright star! I would like to be as beautiful as you are —
Not throwing on the world the ghostly sight of a whore,
As I am, sighing, with my lips wet and sunny,
Like light's inhabitants, a ghastly beach flea.
The moving skies at their insensitive task,
Have poured on me the drops of your luminous mask.
O beautiful light, reverberated in the hands of dusk!
Bright star! If I could have a bit of your radiance,
Not sleep upon the violent breast of my many lovers.
To feel the purity of your glance forever,
Awake in the fever of our astral romance.
Having rendezvous with the empty-feeling death,
Under your illuminating dress — and then cease to breathe.

You will become a song

You will become a song,
When the last chime of the night
Will have carried the light away.
You will become a spark, a wordplay,
A music, fallen ashtray on the land.
A kite escaped from the right hand.
Verses thrown on twilight's band.

Tonight you will become a score,
A fever, a tune, folklore.
New rhymes performed by men older.
Your name will become louder.
During ochre nights, in winter.
My dear I am turning you into a score.

You will become a song; for
I have been humming you all along
The shores of a long spring by the storm.
A song, tonight you shall become,
Yes tonight you will become a classic.
A hit, a tempest born out of music.
— You will become a song.

Poesía sin fin

Santiago, holy city
1940 sprinkled its pain
In slow pinches,
Like charred sugar.
I lived with the sisters;
Lihn Diaz Parra and their peers
Had not yet read me.
At night under the burning sheets,
I'd light a dirty lamp
And gave in to her ideas.

In a macabre enterprise,
She had covered
Every gram of my life,
And captured the music
That slept in my consciousness.
I could only hear her waltzes,
Her dancer's whispers,
Her icy soft words.
She was all the noise
That was missing from my boredom,
All the words with the smell of earth
That weighed reluctant
On my cottony nights,
Standing before the ocean.

My family black cloud
Passed by like an omen,
And Europe lured me
Like a rotten orange.

Poetry is a jaguar

Poetry is a jaguar.
It has bitten our shadows,
And I fall asleep, burning,
In a spiritual forest.
Traveler, a little wine?
Let's drink from the cup of fate;

The dome of the hours awaits us –
Skeptical stars, scattered flowers,
Eternal return of the flames,
Violet ethanol blaze,
Anonymous mooring pontoons,
Adventurers burnt in the flame of History.
Poetry is a jaguar, a wild ounce.
It has devoured our thoughts,
Poetry is a jaguar that watches over our nights;
I waited a hundred days for your voice to reach me.
The horizon suffered the assaults of the morning.
My wound reopened at the sight of the sun.
Today I play whist with the dawn,
My boat crosses the incandescence of morning:
I am a sailor without a captain,
Love is my promised land.

I don't write poetry!

I don't write poetry!
I just pierce the music of silence.
There are bursts of voice, a balloon bounces against a wall.
Rhymes are thrown in front of my eyes.

I don't write poetry!
I simply dilute the night in my broken heart.
I only accompany this woman on the arm of this man,
And in the darkness of their future,
I drop the brightness of some rhymes.
At the level of the ground, love carries them away,
And the wind whispers to me to break the point of my pencil,
On the edge of time that slides like a white dress.

I don't write poetry!
I just borrow the light for a moment,
To bring tears to the cheeks of the bereaved,
I only half-open the door of the home of the dead.

I don't write poetry!
And even if I were to slip my verses
Under the door of despair and loneliness,
Reader, close your eyes on my golden lies,
A star has stolen my ink.

I'm becoming the best poet in town (filaments of fire)

I will become the best poet in this city.
Poetry has burnt the metal of my soul,
One day you walked away on the arm of another.
Don't come near me; I'm haunted by words.
I dilute the ink in the morning blaze
To revive my wounds and make the fire gush
On the paper that floods my unmade bed.

I will become the best poet in this country,
It is a truth melted in the lead of the sky.
I will become the best poet, the most sincere:
Poetry is my fate; poets are my brothers.
They hold my hand at the edge of the twilight.
Don't come any closer! I am contaminated by the ink!
Love has isolated me from men,
And I write with my eyes closed.

I will become the best poet wherever my rage carries me.
It is a vow hung on the windows of the churches and the sky swings.
Don't come any closer! Poetry haunts me; the words alone animate me.
Poetry is a torment that I remake every evening.
The blazing twilight reminds me of my name,
But I remain motionless, fleeing from reason,
The heart blackened by ink, the soul empty of your absence,
And I see the stanzas dancing on the wall
Like filaments of fire.

2

Poetry fever

Paris fever

Thirty-eight caliber on the Champs-Elysées,
A riot police van haunts the dark asphalt,
Acid in the orange juice two streets farther,
Stroboscopes spit a delicious smoke.

I left a tip for the night; she refused it.
The darkness is about to fall into the arms of the day.
Can you hear the first métro approaching?
Shards of glass litter the Champs-Elysées.

My credit card is made of solid gold.
I scratched a Lamborghini on the way in.
My business cards smell of sulphur.
On the bar a rose in a blue vase.

The champagne flutes reverberate the mauve sky.
The silence abandoned the nightclub hours ago.
A beggar wipes his eyes outside
With the first rays of an August sun.

Dresses cut under the pale light.
Dollars rain in the pool full of people.
An insect falls into the plum-flavored liquor.
Rock can be heard until the sidewalk.

The subway station sinks into the night.
Green and pink billboards light up the platform.
The hands of the gold Rolex stop.
I have lit my cigar in the deserted subway car

The fluorescent light of the bars
Calls out to us from the street like a beggar.
An iced coffee please!
I want to keep dancing till morning!

The subway is my dance floor tonight.
Only you and I are swaying between the seats.
The floor is littered with bottles —
Half-drunk and we're off again.

Your lips bleached with cocaine,
Pressed on my sweaty lips,
You've got to look like you're happy
In my city deserted by tranquility.

An escort dressed in a night blue dress
Glides down the avenue like a visa card in a reader.
She has the cold look of a skater
And the smile of a showgirl.

The smoke of the cigarettes envelops us.
Chopped, our voices bewitch the fences.
The grids of the Luxembourg garden answer us by undulating.
That Paris is a flashy façade.

A last bar before the day appears,
The music is crazy; it collides with our eardrums
Like a bee to the walls of a jar.
The rhythm pulses in the four corners of the bar.

Stoned, eyes half closed, drunk,
Waiting for the sun to dry the vodka
And the sweat abandons our wrinkled foreheads.
A security guard has thrown us out into the street.

We walk arm in arm
Before disappearing into an adjacent street.
Light and dark in front of the Triumphal arch,
The Champs-Elysées avenue suddenly lights up

On the Champs-Elysées

I ransacked the boulevard.
My flame thrower lies in a puddle of diesel.
It rains burnt shreds of dollars
On the Champs-Elysées.

I stoned the luxury windows,
Played among the broken glass
While avoiding cutting an artery of myself
On the Champs-Elysées.

I knocked over a police van.
The darkness was blocking my sight.
It smashed itself against a streetlight
On the Champs Elysees.

I — I am the night of the great megacities.
I have taken the shape of every criminal
By carving a shadow worthy of the sky
On the Champs Elysées.

I — I am the night, the night sweat
That invades every square meter,
The back of every stunned visitor
On the Champs Elysées.

I took the form of a herd of teenagers,
Who smoked pot on the sly.
I made them a cradle of shadow,
On the Champs Elysées.

I am the reverse of the bright day,
The infinite nothingness, the insoluble darkness,
That stares at every human form
On the Champs Elysées.

But the morning points at me
Like a haggard criminal.
I stretch out my wrists to the police sun,
That it passes me its luminous handcuffs
On the Champs Elysées.

I have beaten up the night

A brave sun
Went to the police. "I made a mistake," he said,
"I have beaten up the night."

My hot breath
On her cold neck,
I pressed my rays
On her slow black train.

She was suffocating but I
Continued to grab her,
Continued my crime,
A fist of light on her breast.

The cop with round eyes:
"It will be in the papers tomorrow.
Have a glass of gin.
Sleep in a cell."

A shameful sun
Prostrate on a cramped bed,
Memories of bright gardens
Of lovers hand in hand,

Went to the police station
To confess his fault, his crime.
A shady sun
Falls asleep behind bars.

The next day the flashes crackle.
"What are you looking at?"
The night has come to bear witness
In court in her golden cape.

The judge with his round eyes
Watches them hate each other
From one end of the room to the other.
Insults are thrown like stardust.

The night wants her revenge.
She asks for the gallows,
For a violent sun,
For the summer sun.

The district attorney strikes three blows.
The silence—the night falls.
He leaves the courtroom,
The handcuffed sun

Returns to his cell,
Dreaming of a bright moon,
Eyes in the cracks of the ceiling,
Its dark and guilty rays.

"Tomorrow I will be judged
By all humanity,
The one I lit up
The one I burned too much."

"Be merciful, good people.
For I have beaten up the night.
The stars have stained the earth.
Pour me another gin."

"Tomorrow will come with its monstrous train.
I'll go up on the scaffold
With one look back.
I'll melt into the smoke of the sky."

"The red planets
Are already quivering with anger.
Take off these handcuffs.
I'll run away from here."

"I who have beaten up the night
By a summer breeze,
I'm going to melt into the merciful sky
To escape the revenge of the night."

I cut the night with a chisel

Tears of blood on the horizon,
The policeman brutalizes the moon.
I cut the night with a chisel,
A Molotov cocktail in hand.

Clandestine bet, white stars,
Futures dissolved in the tight skies.
The lieutenant kneels near the vault,
Spitting on rose petals on the granite.

My city challenges the Gods to a duel.
A transvestite thief stares at me.
I won the respect of the night,
And I dance with your hideous ghost.

Summer is a serene criminal.
The sun, a haven, a whore,
Reluctantly on the banks,
I put a finger to my lips.

The spans smell of fish and sex.
Los Angeles is forgotten in dark dreams.
Come, I invite you to my condo.
I have a view of the Strip. I have a view of the Eiffel Tower.

Elizabethan dresses, finery of stupor,
The walls have turned white with my despair.
I walk without fear. I scrape the pavements.
My voice carries until the heart of summer.

Tears of blood on the horizon,
The policeman brutalizes the moon.
I cut the night with a chisel,
A Molotov cocktail in hand.

Bird lime (time in prison)

Poem written in Cockney Rhyming Slang

Casting a butcher's hook *(casting a look)*
On the babbling brook
Of her tears,
I raced our old apple and pears *(our stairs).*
Life had removed the syrup of figs *(the wigs)*
And the frontiers
From my ethics.
Every remorse from my north and south *(from my mouth),*
She bid me not to battlecruiser *(don't be a boozer),*
For waiting is harder,
For there will be grief,
And doors always close on a tea leaf *(thief);*
But I, kicked right on my Khyber Pass *(on the ass)*
By her soundness,
Turned to a rock,
Only able to cast a veil of Laugh n Joke *(smoke)*
On her sweet face—until bird lime *(time -in prison-)*
Made her sublime,
A memory,
From the time when I longed for bees and honey *(money).*

The saddest cop in town

LAPD raids Tijuana.
Heroin stained the whitewashed walls.
I threw a baseball into the sun.
I hit the heart of a wounded bird.

The loader of my automatic gun is full.
Let me shoot the evening in vain.
The sun wets my shirt and my Ray-Bans.
The plaster of the sky is falling apart.

A switchblade brandished before the night,
The politician shouted in the church yard.
I drank a case of hooch.
My informant's skull is split in two.

They'll say it's better if it's over between us two.
The radios are crackling, but all I hear is your silence.
Come on, talk to me. I'm disillusioned without your voice.
The waitress is asthmatic, the bar empty without you.

A rum and orange coke two streets over,
Welcome to the Land of Dreams.
Come wallow in hope.
The amusement park turns a blind eye to crime.

And the night flutters, impatient and uncivil.
The iron arms of the future
Have robbed me of your smile.
I punched the cognac balloon.

The ocean blows its silver wind near here.
Come dance a tango with me!
I miss you; talk to me
In this marijuana haze.

I blinked three times.
Pop music tore my eardrums.
The massacre had already happened.
Sirens wailed in the white night.

I'm the saddest guy in the LAPD.
I'm drinking with my eyes open in the police station's bathroom.
The robbers are making eyes at me,
And the ocean swallows my conscience.

The key to my soul I threw in a pool of carbon.
The magazines are all about you and me,
A cop who defied the noise of the megacities.
Get rid of this scandalous rag!

A saxophone player drunk under the moon
Has handed me his silver box.
I'm jogging under the stars.
I'm the saddest cop in town.

Come, meet me on the pier.
I've got some things to say to you before I jump in the waves.
I loved a star; it's gone like a black idea,
And the jazz devours the sky like a fog.

Soccer

It's raining. The grass, the sweat, the noise.
Red. Going to look for God in the stadium.
But who am I? Dust in the eye.
The grass under my cleats.
Am I the reflection of a God on the ball?
Harder, faster. The grass. The sky opens to the light.
Corner. Go for the win!
The horns invade the night in the city.
The stadium shakes. My forehead sweats. I run.
I run away from the noise. The ball bounces on the sun.
Who am I? A God? The sun?
The clouds strangle me.
Am I the spit of an infernal God?
The ball—further to the right. To the left.
It devours the grass like a white fire
Red. My soaked shirt. The noise.
The spectators blow fire in my face
Black. The ball has disappeared into the streamers.
The rain—I run. Fast. Away. Corner.
My breath in the back of another player's neck.
Throw me a deluge of ice water.
My sweat, I'm hot. I run.
On the ground. The grass. The whistle. Quickly.
Does the sun wipes my invisible tears?
Does someone caress my cheek?
The sweat. The sprain. Red. Card.

A thin rain falls. The spectators are grumbling
Agony at the end of the match. The din.
I set the goalkeeper in sight. The grass. White.
Russian roulette. Quickly. I run.
Who am I? Already the grass smells of victory
I run. I run again. Further, quickly. Towards the goal.
The stands rise up like a boa constrictor.
The grass sinks under my cleats.
The cage empties. To the left. To the right. Quickly.
The sky empties itself of its sincere Gods.
The light invades the sky. My face.
The victory—Who am I?

3

World poetry

Istanbul

Smash your dreams, Constantinople,
Hang a smile on your madness,
The 21st century calls you,
It yells, crouched in the darkness
In front of your shattered faces,
That rattle their teeth
Like the singing backwash
Of my memory.
Your mosques? I forgot their pomp;
Hagia Sofia endured too oftentimes
The heavy footsteps of travelers.
The streetcar deviates from its course
In front of a cyan colored mosque
And in a blazing blast.
The speculations on real estate
Trigger protester upsurges.
All these tanks parked in front of
Your scintillating shops,
Do they smell like the roses of Orient
Or chewing-gum and then hell?
Let's not mention your white palace.
Its shadow goes slapping
The banks filled with dust
Of your Levant neighborhood.
The world contemplates your billionaires
Dancing naked on the verge of
Swimming pools flowered with dollars.

Never burned down by the thunder,
Your shady parks are wiped out
Like ideas a bit too virgin,
As soon as the northern wind sprinkles you
With its maritime breath.
Istanbul! I forgot your vivid water
Sliced in the paper of dreams
Under the bold chin
Of your bridges with hollow stomachs.
Their lines dash off until the clouds.
Let's not talk about your wise water.
Byzantium with a past told too many times
I shall come to the oiled shores
Of Bosphorus singing your song.
My guitar expresses every feeling.
I will narrate your deviating stories.
My words are your admirers
Like catamarans at full speed.
I will talk to you about the future
Oh Istanbul, let's not talk about it any longer.
Let me just smoke in your streets.
Unhook the clothes upon us
That hang under the balustrades.
Istiklal avenue weeps their folly,
But Taksim place is ours now.
Ayse Kulin will join us
In the last train but not the last
For your broken city center
And we will cure our amnesia

St Petersburg

I look for a sliver of rose in the ice of St Petersburg,
The reflection of a ghost, the unreachable star.
A tsar pressed my hand. He whispered music to me.
I still hear it from my cloud of hot dreams.

I look for the howling of the bears in the middle of the crowd.
An oil well burns in the opaque desert.
The Nevski perspective is waving under the heat.
I am looking for a sliver of rose in the middle of the summer.

The ice of St Petersburg is a dark mirage,
A dream that I make a hundred times looking for your glance
In the mists of water of life that stink of death,
And I walk quietly, pursued by the hours.

I look for the sun in an icy winter.
Russia has taken my heart and shown it to the beasts.
The night is agitated under an insensitive firmament.
I seek the ghost of the past, the unreachable star.

A ship floats on the Griboïedov canal.
The illuminated bridge lets our dirty heads pass.
The quay has a festive air, a nonchalant look.
The stars parade in their worldly finery.

I still have a few hours to spend in this city,
Looking for a ghost to howl like a bear.
The mafia turns away; I look like a demented angel.
I'm looking for the southern star, the inaccessible torment.

Tibet!

It's a high-altitude dream.
Shangri-La is still amazing.
Here the horses are as intelligent
As the dogs.

And your face floats in the dawn
Like an idea barely touched,
With my fingertips, putting out the candle,
The black smoke from the reddening sky.

The stones pile up in the garden,
And we dance under the awning.
Like a thousand shooting stars,
My memories make garlands in your eyes that hope.

The circular street of Lhasa
Bewitches thousands of pilgrims,
Like us, absorbed in liquid thoughts
Haunted by tomorrow.

A boiling tea spilled
On my lap, and I shouted
A sentence in a sparse dzonghka.
Bring me the Times, so I can make paper airplanes out of it.

But already a procession has come past us
My shoulder still bears the stigma
Of the boisterous and stony winds.
Tibet I'd come back at Mongolian time.

To look for bread in the furnace,
Of summer lying under the feet of the sun,
On the road to Red Feather Lake,
Buddhism has swarmed like a hurried bee,

Like an avalanche of modesty,
Traveler, wait for me on the platform.
When I finish my coffee, I join you.
Let's leave Amdo and go tomorrow.

In the exile of our brick hearts,
The color of sacrifice,
The scent of a closed border,
A gust of independence.

Traveler, let's erase the McMahon line
With chewed gum
And then stick it on the papers,
Place it on the walls of the world.

Tuscany

A cypress hedge in the wind
As if to greet my passage.
I run breathless in the moribund alleys.
The sky shows me its burning fist.

The deep red Chianti of my lips
Still shivers when I hear your name.
The soil is littered with dead bottles.
I'm here, leaning against an advertising sign.

I'm here, alone on the terrace of the Ristoro.
At the castello di Ama, I hear your voice.
It resounds in my conscience
Like the echo of a splendid sun.

And the hills of Chianti
Offer themselves like prostitutes
To the luminous whims of August.
I wait for your shadow in a castle hidden by the clouds.

You see, my love, the night is interrupted
To let us bathe at dusk
In the river that divides Florence
At the end of this steep path.

It sinks into the reds and golds of the evening.
The wind blows your name on the vines.
I bought a dagger and dipped it in Brandy.
I will tear the ochre curtain of the evening.

I will splash a path of light to you.
You see! A child plays soccer.
An old man lights a cigarette.
The sky blows embers on our eyes.

I'll sleep in the abbey
I'll pray, joining our two names
In my prayers like two hands entwined,
The walls of the city of Lucca.

Are the white laces on the night
The Roman theater of Fiesole
Still boasts its history.
It plunges its face into the trees.

Which Gods still listen to me?
I tell you that my fate is done.
It was decided by the olive trees of Tuscany
That bend under the sun like peasants.

And this rain that does not fall!
I wait for you on top of one of the towers of San Gimignano
I spy your shadow hidden between the trees
I will wait for you until it snows . . .

On the hills of Tuscany.

Vienna

Vienna lies in the heart of the Hungarian steppes
A ball was given on the Prater,
A young lady sprained her ankle,
A carriage brings her back in defiance of the rain showers.

Sugar on the lips, under the stucco of the buildings,
The churches of the Innere Stadt *(city center)* mourn the
Habsburgs.
"Wien bleibt Wien" *(Vienna remains Vienna)* even under the
flashes of the tourists,
And the subway rushes by, fanned by the deafening din of its
youth.

All the languages of the Balkans can be heard
In cosmopolitan Vienna, from churches to gothic towers,
To the Sky Café that awaits us on the top floor.
Let's embrace the capital city with a fiery look.

The streets are colorful, luxury hides at every crossroad.
I went to sunbathe in this open-air museum-city; it's summer.
Vienna is a concept store, a cinema passion,
And the giant spire of the cathedral threatens us.

At night—the roller coaster has stopped.
Cotton candy stinks in the air, sweat.
I climbed to the top of the starry night
In a gondola shivering in the rain.

I leafed through the *Times* with a coffee in my hand
In a Kafeehaus *(café)* that dreamed of the past.
The baroque alleys welcome the laughter of children.
Ten little hands clap the air in rhythm.

"Senf oder Kren" *(mustard or horseradish?),*
A Hitler bunker is part of the landscape,
And the rain falls in detuned drops
On the parliament while the night belongs to the ghosts.

I took the pulse of Vienna in a design store.
A colorful house was frightening the grey thickness of the skies.
Put on your skates, Reader, I offer you a lap
On the illuminated and crowded ice rink.

Will you have some more mulled wine while the storm rumbles?
Let's go for a swim in the shimmering water of the Old Danube.
Let's watch Vienna take on its morning colors
From the north tower of St. Stephen's Cathedral,

The Spanish Riding School parades before us.
The specter of Romi Schneider is soaked in light.
He plays the grand piano at night when the Staatsoper *(national opera)* is empty.
Then a ghostly music haunts the capital of Austria.

Montenegro

I don't remember when this dream started. I was on the terrace of the hotel, drinking a lemon Spritz. You took a cab to Podgorica airport; the road was shaking. The road to the airport has many curves, but you were looking at the vineyards, and you were not afraid, you did not even notice the mud nor the rain. I smiled at you and threw my Spritz over the balcony. I think it fell on a cat.

The day splashed on the parade ground of Koto. The monumental winged lion looked at us. I was dizzy, but I didn't drop your hand for a minute, not even when the clock tower jealously threatened us. We entered the cathedral, and the shadows of martyrs danced before the candles. I looked at the shaky stained glass windows; a shower was already falling outside. Then, again, the sun came back to smile at us like a naughty kid.

In the evening, the harbor was crowded, so I took you away from the music to behind a tree. I drove to the old town of Herceg Novi and hugged you in front of the "bloody tower." For a long time, we waited for ghosts to come and ruffle our hair, but only the silence sat with us. I caressed your face for a lengthy time before you wanted to take the road again. The evening fell like my hair on your shoulders, and we took the road again.

Marshal Tito seemed to haunt the minds of the villagers, and the air was moist. I licked an ice cream—what flavor? Probably raspberry—and I put some on your shirt but you didn't notice I am sorry. I wanted to hug you, but I held back because some old ladies playing cards were watching us in an anxious way, as if we would disturb their peace.

The sea finally undressed in front of our love-stunned eyelashes, and we took the boat to cross the strait to Igalo. In Perast, the Venetian palaces reminded us that passion is not the only challenge of beauty and that the skies are sometimes sincere with those who truly are overwhelmed by art and love itself.

I waited until nightfall to take you to make love to me on a private beach, but it was not possible. Many villas were whispering, glasses could be heard clinking, and we ran to escape the prying eyes.

On the way to the hotel, there is a mausoleum that is a little wind-scratched. We passed the hotel and climbed a hill. I was following you; you were walking a little fast. You were becoming the wind, and I was like a twig, lost in you forever.

At the top of that hill, a group of black birds heckled us. The scent of a grilled carp came to haunt our nostrils. I wanted to make love again to you but I could not in front of the villas because walkers filled the picturesque scene before our eyes too soon. I picked a rose, but I didn't have a vase. And so I made a little pile of rocks and scattered the petals on top.

The next day we went swimming in the Tara Gorge; it's a canyon even bigger than the Colorado. I bet you did not know? The light was blinding. The pines perfumed the air. Olive trees swallowed the sun and spat out its fragrant fumes. I bought some oil from a blind merchant. You lay on the sand, and I put two drops on the back of your neck and breathed in your neck.

Behind the beach there was a ruin. Illyrian or Slavic or Turkish lovers came to plunge their desires into it. I took your hand and put it on the rock, and you caressed the old fortress, my hand on yours.

The crimes of the Yugoslav era have left their mark here in the eyes of the sinners. Yet they smile at us as they cast their nets on the turquoise waters. Only the dilapidated buildings hurt the beauty of the landscape here.

My love, don't stop me from going to the Casino tonight; I love to gamble. But I'll tell you a secret: you're my favorite player and the only one I'm willing to lose everything to: life, honor, literature. I gave you my soul on the steep path of the Adriatic coast. Please don't lose it while climbing the thousand steps of the Herceg Novi stairs that lead to paradise.

Under the apricot tree

(Chechnya 1990)

Chechnya. 1990.
Under the apricot tree, it was winter.
I have not forgotten the torn linen shirt
That the officer wore in the middle of the fog,
When he refused to kill us all.

His brown and red frock coat,
The flowers massacred by the din,
Under the apricot tree, it was a flood of light.
The sky was enraged to see us chained to each other.

The officer threw his weapons
Under the apricot tree, among the white flowers;
A man in black shot his refusal. The hamlet was emptied of his soul.
My **pandor** *(musical instrument)* made the stars vibrate.

The grass lost its perfume of violets,
And I buried the officer according to our rites
By the apricot tree, under a rain of white flowers.
I put Brandy in his grave.

A blade of wood was stuck in the ground.
It carried a white and red flame.
The cracks of the grave lamented.
The frost covered the horror, the sky changed color.

The peasants resumed their sowing for God.
The following summer, a shooting contest took place.
Children played on the blue wall, near the apricot tree.
The officer's ghost gave one of them a hand to go down.

The thunder sounded –
The Prince of Kabadie was there too.
His ghost cheered the officer's sacrifice.
The wind was trying to tear off our eyelashes.

The apricot tree cried in the red night,
The warheads fell like sermons.
The mulla hid us in the mosque.
I looked at the sky from the windows—in silence.

The cinema on Lake Baïkal

An open-air cinema
On the banks of Lake Baïkal,
The hero speaks in Buryat.
The dress of the heroine rises
Above a bed of blue flowers,
The ancient district of Aginsk.
The pages of a revolutionary book
Macerate in a golden puddle,
Gorbachev's breath
In the neck of the spectators.
It is an open-air cinema
On the banks of Lake Baïkal.
The Trans-Siberian Railway shelters the fruity dreams
Of a bee and a plate of marmalade,
A sound of wings, the flight of a bird,
Above the Selenga delta.
The grey-blue wolf has invited itself on the banks of the Baïkal.
The dense clouds choke the summer sky.
We play a popular movie:
The hero, machete in hand, on the mountain,
The arms raised to the address of the Gods.
The grey-blue wolf invited himself on the banks of Baïkal.
The apricot trees are in bloom.
The Trans-Siberian Railway shelters the winged sighs
Of a fly and a glass of milk,
The quivering of the water, the black forest.

A sunbeam has fertilized the earth,
Your black eyes, the immense sky,
And before the screen stretched between us,
The people of Baïkal are watching a film.

The snow on Coney Island

I dove off the Staten Island ferry
In an oily mud.
The sunset inspires me this poem,
A breath between two towers,
And I join you to take you away from the night,
The shiver of a cloud.
The vertigo is post-industrial.
The barber points at me.
My chewing gum is becoming a ghost,
A derelict warehouse.
A young boy with a bright yellow spray in his hand
Stumbles down one of the 154 stairs of the Hudson Yards.
The steps hold the remnants of summer
And all the leaves fall, dead and weary.
Catch me if you can.
I'll run till I lose my breath
In the middle of your laughter.
It's dark but the neon lights catch the eye.
The images are twitching 24/24.
In the antechamber of our consciousness,
I'll run until my heart gives out
And the magpies tear out my eyes.
Here the elms are in flower.
They sing softly, so that we leave them in peace,

A prayer for Manhattan,
A flashy sign
Has come down and the wind lifts it
Into the farthest clouds.
A small church vomits its worshippers
On a crowded street.
If you want to find me
Come and look for me in the cloister
Near the Metropolitan Museum of Art.
I sew a scarf of dreams
In the hope of seeing the snow again
On Coney Island this winter.

Dublin's flames

Airlink 747 shuttle from Paris,
Dublin stretches like a lousy dog.
Your reflection ripples on each of these clouds,
A wall of steam over our dirty necks.

A stop further at O'Connell Street,
I get off in front of Christ Church Cathedral.
Passers-by jostle me.
My coffee spills on the dark asphalt.

Meet me on the banks of the Liffey.
Let's light up every grey-green cloud
With our fingers full of black magic.
Let's light up the night with our slender fingers.

The City Hall insurgents
Control the access to Dublin
And haunt the twists and turns of history.
Can you hear their cries?

Along the Docks and the Grand Canal,
I chew a plastic straw.
The ground is littered with corpses
Of green and gold bottles.

Join me in this closed theater.
We'll make the city howl with joy.
Let's rekindle the flame in the eyes of the actors
Of the city of Dublin.

Dun Laoghaire, the village by the sea,
Will welcome our thirsty hearts.
Let us quench our thirst with the foam.
Let's quench our passion with the ocean's fire.

Merrion square, a tramp awaits the rain
Bathed in the full August sun.
The cathedrals shade the happiness.
Let's pray before we sell our souls.

The capital city of the Republic of Ireland
Holds out paper arms to us
And an open fire.
Our tears dry up on the cobblestones.

I spent the night untying
The chains of a ghost of Trinity College.
He gave me a rose of sulphur
To thank me for delivering him.

And his cries still echo
All the way to the Bank of Ireland.
The bundles of banknotes are jingling
To the sound of this dreamy din.

The House of lords is deserted.
Come on, let's go! Let's collect the gold dust.
Let's take possession of the scenery.
Let's take a member's seat for the night.

The Speaker of the House
Will not hold it against us.
He lies in the arms of a woman of the night,
Half asleep away from politics.

The battle of the Boyne
And the siege of Londonderry
Wiped out the last political glory,
And the city sinks into the dust.

I made myself a crown of shamrocks
And drank all the water of the Liffey
That my heart could hold;
Traveler and I breathed your memory.

The city cradles us in its sunny arms.
Come play cricket with me.
Run faster if your heart can.
My legs can handle the speed.

The Taoiseach has beautiful eyelashes.
Let's make her promise to come back
to Haunt the government building at night.
Let's share a kir champagne with her

The Olympia theatre is blindfolded
And hopes to survive the fires
That the actors have lit
In their incendiary monologues.

The City Hall insurgents
Control the access to Dublin
And haunt the twists and turns of history.
Can you hear their cries?

The capital of the Republic of Ireland
Holds out its paper arms
And an open fire
Our tears dry up on the cobblestones

4

Multilingual poetry

Aashra—a flowerless garden

(Sudanese Arabic and English)

*[Sudanese Arabic is the variety of Arabic spoken in Sudan and some
parts of Eritrea by roughly 31.9 million speakers]*

1 **Wahid** – I am a sailor without a ship,
And the storm shakes the sea of my ideas.
On the pontoon my heart flies in the dark night,
The stars shine on the ocean of my soul.

2 **Itneen** – And your face floats above the foam
Like a bird, immobilized by my love,
Your smile is my rudder, thunder has struck a wave
And I paddle tirelessly towards the red sun

3 **Talata** – Three stars form a trio of luminous mist
Mathematics has no hold on the ocean,
Here the calm returned, I plunged my hand in the waves,
And my heart froze in the swirl of black water

4 **Arbaa** – I am a bird forgotten by the sky,
My compass sends flashes in the moist air
East-south-north-east, your smile made me lose sight of the horizon
And the sea whitens in my path

5 **Khamsa** – I am this child who looks at me in the distance,
And this old man who greeted the departure of my imaginary ship
By shrugging his shoulders, he who has seen so many men
Become mad for love

6 **Sitta** – I am a sailor without a boat, an angel without God,
The night took possession of the sails of the sky,
And I split the future with my invisible bow
I am the sailor haunted by the memory of the ocean

7 **Sabaa** – Seven times, I pronounced your name,
A seagull landed on the ropes which slipped into the sea,
I chased it away, shouting a psalm
But once it flew away, it did not leave me out of sight

8 **Tamaniya** – I am a lighthouse forgotten on a beach,
I am a feeling unknown to men,
I am the sand that comes to wet itself with your oceanic steps
Waiting for you to take me in your liquid arms

9 **Tisaa** – I am the ninth day of the Creation,
God was absent, a rose took control of the world,
The morning cleared up splashing your face with light,
God was absent and the ocean took my courage

10 **Aashra** – I am a garden without flowers,
An abandoned lighthouse—a living room without a clock,
And I speak to the ocean of time as to an old friend,
He who pushes me towards the shore of love

Dronnigens tale / A Queen's speech

(Danish and English)

[Danish is a North Germanic language spoken widely in Denmark, Greenland and the Faroe Islands by about six million people]

Dronningens tale starter *(The Queen's speech begins).*
Let's run before the rain tears the black knife of the night.
It's raining cotillions. The rain is dancing around our necks.
A television has been installed in the hairdressing salon.
A woman sweeps with the broom while listening to the sweet
voice of her Majesty.

Kom, sid ne dog tag et glas champagne *(Come, sit down and have a glass of champagne).*
Let's watch our hopes drown tonight in the river.
With the help of alcohol, our torn hearts separate from our chest
And fly away to the dazzling firmament of the skies.
A cloud sucks our eyes. The light explodes. A young woman passes by.

Du er fri til at gøre hvad du vil *(This year has not been easy).*
I had to pray to the devil, I who am a poor soul.
I had to throw away my cards. They told the truth about our destinies.
They had scared me. They had betrayed me,
And the demons danced before my exhausted body.

Hvor var det en fin tale *(That was a really nice speech)*.

Come on, let's go set a police car on fire.
Before the mafia takes over the heart of Copenhagen.

Come, give me your hand, take my drink. Cast the booze over these flowers.

Let's run before the rain tears the black knife of the night.

Mishaq / The Game

(Hebrew and English)

[Hebrew is the official language of Israel and is spoken by roughly 8.3 million residents]

I long to find happiness in the **shalvah** *(serenity)* of this poem.

I played chess with fate, the most beautiful **sahqan** *(player)* in this neighborhood.

Tzohorayim *(midnight)* already, the night is ringing at my door.

I'll go to the next **mitzpor** *(bird watching post)*. I'll fly away.

I'm going to damn myself in the dunes of **Mitzrayim** *(Egypt)* to the sources of black magic.

I will change my skin, change my face, pour my blood in the burning sand.

I will finally be yours in this cradle of light, every night, **malakh** *(my angel)*.

The dawn will break. I'll go back to the dunes to melt into the sand.

The evening lifts my **levanah** *(white)* dress.

Tzohorayim *(midnight)* already, the night is ringing at my door.

I cried more than usual tonight, but I had to resolve to abandon the earth.

You are **hofshi** *(free)* my love. I give you your freedom.

May the **horèf** *(winter)* take away your beautiful face.

As for me I return to dust.

A **heikhal** *(palace)* of sand will welcome my body.

A tornado approaches. I will try to melt into it.

I played chess with fate, the most beautiful **sahqan** *(player)* of this neighborhood.

I long to find happiness in the **shalvah** *(serenity)* of this poem.

The Red Bird

(Pashto, Dari and English)

[Pashto and Dari are the two main languages of Afghanistan and are respectively spoken by roughly 13 and 9 million residents]

(Pashto)

Chwaschina em *(I am sorry)* for my lies
I just wish your smile would fly away like the embers
If you still have love for me,
Mehrabani wokra da wolika *(please write it down somewhere)*
On a sheet of cigarette paper or on the ground
I proposed to you in front of a **pewleys** *(policeman)*
His face was stained with dust, his eyes
Were shadowed with the past. I pressed his hand into mine.
In Kabul as names became graves

(Dari)

Let's go to another country
The road will be **schajad** *(perhaps)* our last asylum,
The sky shows us the way, it sighs infinitely above our human morals
Your hair smells like **yaasaman** *(jasmine)*
I'll breathe your neck until I go mad
I'm running out of money, I'm left with no wine.
And Kabul lights up under the fighting

(Pashto)

One language is not enough
I will trace our names in Pashto and Dari on the walls
The shadows pass by, I thought I saw the flash of an AK47 close by.
In the night of blood, the red bird flew through Kabul.
You see this **sanema** *(cinema)* under the rubble
I think the ghost of an old actor invites us to join him
And the **baran** *(rain)* of his words falls on the movie screen
The weather is **weraz** *(cloudy)* the red bird is watching us

(Dari)

Follow me into the garden of the emperor Babur,
Take my hand in the **Bâgh-e Wafâ** *("the garden of loyalty")*
Let your **shaal** *(shawl)* wrap the flight of the red bird
He will bring it back to you with magical patterns
The ghosts of old women
Who died under the bombs while having tea
Laugh and invite us to converse with them,
My love, take my hand, let's go.

(Pashto)

I proposed to you in front of a a **pewleys** *(policeman)*
His face was stained with dust, his eyes
Were shadowed with the past. I pressed his hand into mine.
In Kabul as names became graves
Za la ta sara meena kawom *(I love you)*
But the Taliban have stormed the endless night
Close your hand on the light of a star!
It will protect you from fate

(Dari)

You see, this **sitara** *(star)* has begun to shine, no it's not a warplane
Your eyelashes closed out of exhaustion.
Forgive me for my lies,
Come, we must keep moving
Through the rubble, the godless sky,
Forget our memories,
Man nami dâtam *(I don't know where we will be tomorrow)*
One day we'll be back dancing like crazy in the gardens of Kabul.

(Pashto)

Za la ta sara meena kawom *(I love you)*
But the Taliban stormed the endless night
Yawazi mee pregda! *(leave me alone)!*
Never! Close your hand on the light of a star
It will protect you from fate
Come and dance in the only bar still open tonight
The river of the city is a dance floor,
Neon lights are hanging on the mausoleums

Davvin / In the North

(Sami language of Sápmi and English)

[Sami languages are spoken by the Saami people in Northern Scandinavia by almost 35,000 people]

From the heart of Sweden to the Kola Peninsula,
Snow falls on the gas station.
The highways look like starry skies.
A **joik** *(traditional song)* is heard on the radio.

The great lake is inhabited by a thick smoke
Which raises its white hands to the sky.
There is coal in the eyes of the fishermen.
The fishes are the souls of the damned.

The birch bark displays both our names.
The forest is adorned with a purple sheet. It is the winter sky.
I asked the stars to pour me water.
It rained on the territory of Sápmi.

The **boazu** *(reindeer)* stopped at the edge of the village.
He looked at the moon in the clouds.
Then he galloped towards the horizon
And disappeared while I mourned your departure.

He joined a black herd, stuck to his fellow creatures.
His gaze sunk in the starry vault.

He forgot the wild humanity in the tundra,
And I fled from the companionship of men.

I pitched my **goahti** *(tent)* in the forest.
Davvin *(in the north)* the rain falls hard;
Every drop is a liquid dagger,
And my tears freeze on my cheekbones.

It is an **ahkidis muitalus** *(a sad story)*,
A journey to the invisible eternal.
I rise every morning with the dawn,
And the forest smiles and speaks to me.

Johtti *(traveler),* I live alone in the forest.
The reindeer keep me company.
I have given up taming the birds,
And the rain washes away my dark thoughts.

Can you hear the sun yawn?
I cut a shiny tree trunk,
The chips are glowing on the wet earth.
I will make the horizon blaze.

Mina olen. . . My name is. . .

(Estonian and English)

[Estonian is a language of the Finnic branch spoken in Estonia by about 1.1 million people]

Good evening, Mr. Poet
What is the use of your fingers that slide on the night
As on the sable coat of a passer-by
My hands only grasp the dust of the evening
I am an angel curled up in a nave of silence

Mina olen viletsus *(My name is "misery")*
Parliament has forgotten my face
My pain has the depth of the Baltic Sea
Will you find my body immersed in the snowy body of the river
Emajõgi
I have turned into a curse

Good evening, Mr. Poet
Will you make the horses of your conscience dance
In the blue landscape of the taiga
I am hungry, give me a **piruka** *(Estonian pastry)*
Do not plunge your eyes into the misery of the night

Mina olen unustus *(My name is "oblivion")*
Are you crying? Why did you stop?
Usually silence makes my torn blouse swell

Tallinn awakens in a half-moon sun
Give me your hand let's walk together on the ramparts

Good evening, Mr. Poet
What good is the moon shining on your pale face
Vabandust *(excuse me)* would you have some money
Hunger is a conscientious friend
She is faithful and eats out of my hand

Mina olen pimedus *(My name is "darkness")*
The stars have stolen the light from my eyes
The houses here stand out
Like orange slices on the sky
And the threatening shadow of the police runs along the wall

Thank you, Mr. Poet
For this night of snowstorm in the shelter of your poetry
Hand in hand on the walls of the castle of Kadriorg
I will remain prostrate in the darkness like a small dirty dog
The Marguerite tower lights up, I think I love you

Fréttamynd / The journalist

(Icelandic and English)

[Icelandic is a North Germanic language spoken by about 314,000 people mostly in Iceland where it is the official language]

I made a deal with the Gods of this country;
They will let me do a **fréttamynd** *(report)* here.
If I serve them a **drykkur** *(drink)* of light
And a black currant kir mixed with champagne,
I made a deal with the Gods.
A little paper **bylting** *(revolution)*,
I am the writer of the Gods.
Meet me in my silver **lyfta** *(lift)*
Before this world goes up in **reykur** *(smoke)*.
A **sendiherra** *(ambassador)* read my article.
He dipped his fat lips in whiskey.
The **klukka** *(clock)* announced midnight.
The ghost of a **tónskáld** *(composer)* appeared;
He made a silent bow to us.
A single **stjarna** *(star)* shone behind his shoulder
Through the open window, in the forgetful night.
I made a deal with the Gods here.
An invisible **svanur** *(swan)* accompanies me everywhere
In the asphalt **sundlaug** *(pool)* of Reykjavik.
I question the witnesses of each life,
And every life seems to me a mystery to be taken seriously.
I question every blade of grass, every God.

The children of the country look at me whispering,
What **hammingja** *(happiness)* to work with them.
I am the journalist of these hills,
The narrator of these dusty palaces,
The editor of every line of sky,
And my life is a **dómkirkja** *(cathedral)* of ink
That flows and flows into the river of the future,
Carrying with it the **hringur** *(ring)* of sobriety.
I am the writer of this country's laughter,
And I have made a deal with the deities here.
They'll let me shoot their enchanted talks,
If I burn after each of my footages,
So that the smoke makes them a vaporous cloak.
The **himinn** *(sky)* is witness to my wish.
I am the only journalist accepted by the Gods.

Bizitzak aurrera jo du noski /
Of course, life went on

(Basque and English)

I was walking on the blue hill
On my **itsasorako** promontory *(with a view of the sea)*
The red and golden train of the Rhune passed me
The wind blew dead leaves on my face
And on a rock I saw sitting thoughtful
A friend who was gazing at the Atlantic
I took his calloused hands, he stood up
He showed me the delirious flight of the clouds

A woman's face shone in the sky
The night suddenly slapped us on the back
Like an old acquaintance
My friend's beret flew off

A cesta punta player caught it
« **bizitzak aurrera jo du noski!** » *(of course, life went on!)*
My friend said to me, his eyes misty with tears
But where is she, tell me?

The stars began to tremble
Love seemed to me an implacable adversary
I took my friend away from the cliff of the Basques
The wind blew an icy rain on our cheeks

He showed me the luminous parade of boats in the cove of
Saint-Jean-de-Luz
And whispered to me softly
But where is she, tell me?
I lost her for ever.

I was walking on the blue hill
The sun for all companion
When I came across an old friend
Sitting on a rock and crying over the Atlantic

The red and gold train of the Rhune was already moving away
The night gave us a slap on the back
And the fire of our conversation kept us awake
« **bizitzak aurrera jo du noski!** » *(of course, life went on!)*
My friend, his eyes filled with tears, kept asking me
But where is she, tell me?
The stars began to tremble
The night swayed between light and shadow
« **zuhaitzak oraindik zut dirau askatasunaren gogoz** » *(the tree
still stands proudly in memory of freedom)* I shouted to the moon
But my friend kept crying
Where is she, tell me?
I think I have lost her for ever
I answered him with a shrug:
« She is in the wind that haunts your wet eyes,
In your supple wrist when you put verses on paper,
In the dew that covers the grass of the gardens of the Abbadia castle
In the cement that walls our coasts

She is everywhere, she is part of you
And that's why I love her too »

— « What, you my friend, do you love her?! »
You, whom I thought was my dearest confidant? »
« Without knowing her, your friend, I love her
Because she is now part of our friendship,
Of the nights you will live in the future to make her face revive
In the sands of your soul

I love her too since she is in your heart,
And since you are my dearest friend
Your heart my friend is my dearest friend
That is why I love her without knowing her »

« But you don't understand, » he answered, wavering,
She is not a part of me
She is everything that loves outside of me
A bird that loves the sky
Wine that loves the cup
A priest who loves the nave of his church
The night that loves the poets
The earth that loves the travelers

Eguzkia agertu zen hodei arteik, inoiz baino ederrago *(the sun
reappeared between the clouds, more beautiful than ever)*
We had talked all night
And the trees seemed to touch the pink base of the clouds
And talk among fools like us!
« **bizitzak aurrera jo du noski!** » *(of course, life went on!)*
I walked down the blue hill
I could still hear the voice of my friend
But where is she, tell me?
The stars began to tremble
He was still walking beside me

A young woman in a red dress passed us
She had taken the golden train from the Rhune

The dawn made a fiery trail for her
« **amildegitik behera jaurtikiko nauzue!** » *(you will precipitate me in the abyss)*
Shouted my friend charmed by her smile;
She passed us,
Then he began to sing again,
Then he turned back to me
And the stars shone above us
« **bizitzak aurrera jo du noski** » *(of course, life went on)*

5

A game of love. . .

You are like water

You are like water,
Cooled, untroubled miles of glittering cover,
And I am like a hundred suns
In their always burning runs.

You are like the earliest water
From the sky deep down on earth,
Reaching you on one rare event
I see you dry in one moment,
And when you reach me up there,
In your arms I feel the intensity of care.

But you leave. And I die from surviving you.
Water—You are
The very water on the corner of my mouth
When I kiss you. Pure and refreshing touch
That takes my heart to wetness,
Water from my inner self,
Virgin and frivolous,
Necessary element.

Every day the sun rises to light you
Without ever saying I love you.

You are like the earliest water
From the sky deep down on earth,
Reaching you on one rare event.

I see you dry in one moment,
And when you reach me up there,
In your arms I feel the intensity of care.

I shall be like the ocean's only sun,
Powerful but vain,

And you are like a hundred drops
Filling my eyes with water's ropes,
Escaping from me into life moves,
And I ask myself seeing you from above –

You are like the earliest water
From the sky deep down on earth,
Reaching you on one rare event.
I see you dry in one moment,
And when you reach me up there,
In your arms I feel the intensity of care.
Shall the sun cry you over?
I think you have the answer.

Chess game against the Gods

There was a granite stud
Near the pier,
A low table weakened
By the gusts and the salt.

The sun was lighting
The edges of the waves.
A few sprays
Wet my white lashes.

I searched the horizon,
Where was the flash of my youth,
The liquid flesh of my wife,
Her white gold wrists?

My cap fell to the ground.
I thought I saw the silhouette
Of a God in the storm
On the table, near the granite block.

A glass chess set
Flickered.
Like a broken neon sign,
I hastened.

As the storm roared,
I moved each pawn,
Like languid beliefs
Carefully

My serene opponent
Burned the horizon
With his thermogenic eyes.
I had this vision

Of a sudden indentation
Tearing the pearly sky,
I hummed the song she loved,
While playing chess with Providence.

I'm just a poor fellow,
A patriarch haunted by his infirmities.
I've been working all these years
In a boredom-laden slum.

I was a locksmith in a town
Unimportant and often
I prayed to God to give me back
The one I loved, if he would.

I want the morning to resurrect my widowed heart,
But every morning laughs in my face.
I found nothing new
Except the next day.

I clutched only bitterness and cold
Against my scrupulous chest.
The beautiful ones slammed the door of my store
By throwing banalities in my face.

In my face, I dreamed
One day to defy the stars,
To see my wife's smile again,
The caress of her dirty clothes.

But every cloud bursts with laughter.
A black gull takes bets.
I am drunk with iodine and rage.
Can you hear the foam ignite?

With his windy arms God spurs
The king towards the nearest square.
I swallow a mucus, wrinkle my misty forehead:
The game is far from being won.

Above our fight,
A goddess troubles the incarnate sky.
She dances at the sight of the shining pieces,
Laughs and elbows me.

Her eyes pierce the wall of my consciousness.
Her tongue licks the bottom of my ears.
I hear a whisper in the cold.
Her tongue seems to have frozen with joy.

She has Angelina's eyes,
The same heavy lashes, the same voice,
Ah, if my wife could see us,
The Goddess, the chess set and me.

I played with her all night,
On the table by the pier,
Soaked in this drunken clarity,
Defying an eternal opponent.

Tying up all the momentum of life in me,
Against impatient Okeanos I brandished
Every flicker of humanity
To stay in the game.

I did not lower my eyes until the morning.
Checkmate to the Eternal,
My cap flew off!
The foam caught up with it—or was it Her?

My eyes struck by the light
Slipped from their earthly orbit.
I slumped to the ground,
Like a sandblasted mountain.

Already the sun is up.
Men and women are murmuring.
A little girl lowers my eyelids,
But behind the crowd I see my wife—resurrected.

Snow of ideals

I walked in a snow of ideals barefoot.
The day fell into the arms of the night,
My book under my arm, seeking my salvation
In the light that slanted on the luxury stores.

I dropped a page in the snow, I think.
I think it was a poem; it contained my pain.
It spoke of the purple arena that we call evening's skies,
Of the light whitening benches and bums.

A black sheet was thrown over our day-bent backs.
The stars flashed like misaligned neon lights.
The snow disappeared in the bitter darkness,
And my lips whispered this final prayer.

I cried, and my tears traced your name in the snow.
The boulevard haunted my eyes with its cold streetlights.
God had disappeared into another megalopolis.
I was afraid to lose you, I recited a prayer.

A game of love

I played cards with the devil.
He bet that I would lose.
We were perched on a mountain
Surrounded by flaming torches.

I played cards with the devil.
He whispered in my ear
That he would not rip off my soul if he won;
The sayings were wrong about that.

I started to shuffle the cards.
The devil demanded my heart if he won.
He would not rip off my soul if he won;
The sayings were wrong about him.

He told me he loved me.
All he asked for was my heart,
If he won in the depths of the eternal snows,
That he would only take my life, my blood,

That he would make me his wife.
I dealt the cards one by one,
Looking at him stealthily.
His smile set the mountain on fire.

We spent a night playing.
The moon lit up our cards.
He was so focused.
He didn't realize I was watching him.

I played cards with someone
Who haunts the Bible and wine.
I played cards with someone
Hated all over the world.

The mountain turned pale in the morning.
I dealt the first draft.
The devil was crying like a wounded bird.
I was close to winning.

The mountains began to tremble,
And the torches went out.
I was about to lay down my last card
When suddenly, I was taken by a dizzy spell.

I threw it into the wind;
The wind plunged it into a canyon.
I looked up; the Devil was bleeding.
I embraced him to my tanned chest.

We had spent a night playing.
The moon had lit up our cards.
He was so focused
That he didn't realize I loved him.

The photophore

Take me to vibrate in **Yurikamome** ("the laughing gull').
My soul is futuristic, burned by a hundred neon lights.
The luminous panels slap my shameful conscience.
Already the stores close; the night opens its beating doors.
The lute constellated with our eyes, reflects our blue dreams.

The Rainbow bridge protects our eyes from the darkness,
An amusement park with blue reflections,
The shameful exuberance beads on Sunshine city,
Reflects the soul of the sky; the oxygen of the city dies,
And the waters of the rivers reveal their gloved hands.

Take my hand, traveler. Let's enter that deserted nightclub.
Give me that gin; I've burnt too much without you.
The tower of Tokyo penetrates the stellar vault
And pierces the mystery of our wandering silhouettes.

A color is lacking

If there is a God on earth,
Please let him remove all
The blue color of my life
And the sky of my nights.

The blackness grabs me by the throat
When I see the clouds
Swimming in this error.
Remove this color.

This hue of horror,
Of plastic in the seas,
The antithesis of red,
This color disturbs me,

And my heart turns white
At the approach of the night.
For I cannot find you
Looking at this color.

The skies have betrayed me,
And your life misses you,
One color less,
A morning with a brown sky.

It's not much
But to give me back my life,
My life overturned, deserted
Wasted without you.

Dismiss the blue crime case.
Give the sea for dead.
Thus the sky perhaps
Will return you to the earth.

The mountain of soul

I cut the mountain in stone all night long.
I built a bridge over the hours, a bewitched bridge.
The ivy sealed the fate of my work, and I waited for you to cross it.

I am going to the mountain.
The birds have fallen silent. The wind no longer blows.
The sun has burned the night; it has become shredded.
Will you think of me? I am going to the mountain.
Will you think of me when I contemplate,
At the top of the pink clouds,
Our cities spread out in a pale darkness?
Love is a sea of dreams, but
How can I survive without the sea?
How can I not get hurt while lying in the icy snow?

I left this morning, without anything, taking the wind with me.
I crossed the city, the glowing companies, the forest, the valleys.
Your smile dazzled in me every time I met another soul.

God, the mountain was beautiful. It suddenly appeared to me;
It looked up at the sky like a proud dancer.

I clutched my hand to my chest.
I felt pain. A bird (or was it the reflection of my fear?) stroked my face;
I walked steep paths. I got lost a hundred times,
And it is thirsty, desperate; it is there
That the ice creature stood before my dark eyes,
Like a fallen angel awaiting the right moment to devour my soul.

With my hands in the melted snow, I cried;
Then I laid down on a bed of moss.

The wind caressed my face like a sincere friend.
My eyes closed. I saw your smile again.

You never knew where I went.
The avalanche covered my burning body.
You never knew who placed in front of your closed door
These million verses, which were intended for you.

Consider that it was the wind, which gave you the gift.
I never knew if he was my friend
Or if he was laughing at my soft heart.

Take these verses, if one day you too,
My love, take the same road as me
To the mountain of soul,
For a stronger, a less vain lover than me.

These words will be the flames which will keep you alive.
May they light your way
And the impotent moon
On its perch of wrought iron,
Observes your journey,
And once you reach the top,
May you recover your lost smile.
May your heart be warmed.

As you see our city illuminated below,
The clouds stroking you in a dreamy ballet,
The flowers opening their corollas, and the mosses caressing you,
Then you'll realize that this life was real,
And without knowing how you stayed alive,
You'll make your way back to our neighborhood; yes,

Yes, the mountain was beautiful.
But it was only an impatient dream.
My love, run away from the danger of its company.
Come and take the dawn in your bright palms,

And one day, embracing the one you will marry,
You will gaze at the snowy peaks
From the roof of your terrace.

At this point in your life, think of me who disappeared on a winter
morning,
Who was your friend and still loves you from her night.
My ashes are mixed with the eternal snow,
And I've been watching you for a long time,
From the heart of the icy flowers of the mountain of soul.

Adrift

I tore a Bible to shreds, blood stained the foam,
And I let myself be carried away by the raging currents.
A column of mist rose up in front of the bow of my ship.
The night appeared like a brilliant idea.

I caressed the black cloak of the skies with my half-closed eyes.
God the sea was hypnotic, in its liquid coat.
The foam of the waves tangled with my ideas.
I howled with laughter at the irrepressible flight of clouds.

The arms in cross, on my raft, my tears buried in the water,
I prayed to God to give me a course, and I spat onto the ocean.
The light of a star guided me; a thought followed me like a shadow.
I was stalked by your image, reflected in the night and the waves.

The garden of our silences

I have entrusted myself to the clouds,
They who too often stare at us
Without touching with their cloth,
The gardens of our silences.

I will go and tell the twilight
That the rain has failed me.
I watered with my bare hands all evening
My roses and I am exhausted.

You see, this child in the garden,
It's a mirage; he's a hundred years old.
He comes to play blind man's bluff with the wind
And chew the thorns of the roses.

Silence haunts the palms of my hands.
Near the pond, a swan in my garden
Turned into a geyser of smoke.
The passers-by looked at it in wonder.

Let me rest for a moment
In this garden by this pond.
Let me convince the flowers
That solitude makes me happy.

Night hides in the sleeves of day.
The fabric of light is thicker than ever.
August lectures the rain that comes and goes
Like a friend a little too sincere.

See, the twilight lingers on my arms.
It makes me an ochre and white cradle,
A parenthesis of joyful light
That spreads through the pupils of the evening.

And this child in the garden,
He is a spectre; he is a thousand years old!
He comes to play tarot with the night
And argues with the stars.

6

History's withered roses

1914

The City of Light in the fog,
The airplanes shade it.
The parasols of the damsels caress the sun.
The war knocks at the doors.

The youth are mobilized.
1914 year sung at the piano forte.
The Belle Epoque turns its heels.
The war knocks at the doors.

A priest on a bicycle through the fields,
The Sacré Coeur basilica takes the sun.
God has deserted the Champs-Elysées.
The war knocks on the doors.

Pierre Loti returned from Iceland.
France has its fingers dipped in ink.
The Dreyfusards read Poil de Carotte.
The war knocks at the doors.

The National Society of Music
Gives a concert for posterity.
The Internationale is whispered.
The war knocks at the doors.

Art nouveau teases the souls.
Action française sets fire to the powder keg.
The newspapers talk only about the Tour de France.
The war knocks at the doors.

A politician shows his fists
To the golds of Palais-Bourbon,
And the storm spits on Paris.
The war knocks at the doors.

I have something to say!

I have something to say, but I don't know what—
Fifty years ago incandescent graffiti
Were bleached by the morning dew.
The insults stimulated the violence
Of a light boiling with rage:
Minimum wage 2.2 *francs* per hour,
Paid vacations in Eure-et-Loire.

The Sorbonne crumbles under a rain of steel.
Who can fall in love
With a 5% growth rate?
Vaneigem did let escape from his dark pen
A treatise on learning to live
For the use of young generations.

His mythologized teenage audience
Absorbs the windy spaces of the capital,
Forfeited the teleguided figures,
Frozen in a haughty economism,
Shot down the eagle that subdued idealism
Of its concupiscent talons.

Those who make revolutions by halves
Only dig themselves a grave –
And freedom is the crime
Which contains all the crimes.
The walls had the word.

In a smoky studio of the Beaux-Arts
600,000 silk-screened posters
Hatch in stylized buds in May
On the rain-damaged walls.

Under the cobblestones, the beach,
American way of life, mirages on the fly,
In June in the Luxembourg park,
A young advertising man lights up the night
By lighting a Chesterfield
With a member on strike of the
French anti-riot police.

At the other end of the planet
Ho Chi Minh shakes its bloody sky
On the helpless belly of the planet.
Dazzled by the incarnate shards,
The rebels bludgeon with their cries
The established authority.

The walls have been whitewashed.
The posters disappeared.
The cobblestones have become the sand
Of Paris beach—my city extends its frozen blandness,
In July and August History settled down.

Revolution

Let me leave this city,

The revolution is the wind swollen with sky that rises on our eyes.
Petals of regrets fall on our lips.
The ghosts have stormed the Pantheon tonight.
Let me pass through this cloud of angry souls,
These brown cohorts, these bitter cohorts;
The people who see the truth melt under the sun,
Their wrinkled hands clutching the hand of hope,
I lifted my ambition above my brow; it burned like a flame in the
evening.

Let me desert the wind, leave my country,
Abandon the palaces, the cities—Revolutionary songs,
Lick the cobblestones of Paris.

The upset notes shook the waves of the Seine.
The ghost of Victor Hugo bathed in a dark puddle
And humiliated me while I ran out of breath
As I betrayed freedom through the evening light.
See that angry cloud near the Champs-Elysées?

Truth rose like a neglected lover.
I raised my eyes on the night; it poured courage on me.

I return as a hero with my hands buried in the clay of the capital city.
A ghost haunts the bottom of my eyes.

The streets are full of victorious demons.
I saw the specter of Jaurès kneeling near a church.
He spoke to me of a bygone era and I retreated.

The truth embraced me. We danced on the lit platform.
We danced in the light of utopia. We had Paris dance.
Tomorrow will come with its dark bridal train.
We will abolish the oppression, this gloomy star,

Eleanor of Aquitaine

Queen of France and England,
Her fine fingers beat the measure.
A troubadour sings in the langue d'oc.
A magician sends doves to hell.

Elder daughter of the Duke of Aquitaine,
Courtly love, the radiance of the language
Are only the reflection of the medieval sun.
The dresses are heavy, the steps hurried.

Tapestry workshops are created.
Wedding night in the castle of Taillebourg
Macabru is sent away from the court
For having sung his love to the queen.

Eleanor offers her husband
A vase made of rock crystal
Given to her grandfather
By the taifa king of Saragossa.

The second crusade on the march,
Eleanor returns alone by boat.
Abandoned by Louis VII,
Her ship is taken in a battle.

The black legend of the queen of Aquitaine,
Her ghost in the clouds of History,
Jean de Salisbury traces her name on the yellowed paper.
The cathedral of Poitiers owes its life to her.

The abbey of Fontevraud under the rain,
Her tombstone awaits us; the colors have survived.
In her wrinkled hands, the Book of Life
The queen will read each day of her death.

Voynich's manuscript

It is a fist of light in the night.
A Franciscan monk
Crumpled the parchment page
On which a herbarium was blooming.

A merchant of old books recovered it.
1912 the war is at the gates of Europe.
Wilfrid Voynich lost a life
Deciphering yellowed pages.

In the library of Yale
The students flow like fresh water.
Is it an alchemists' herbarium?
The night pierces the heavy wooden windows.

It is a fist of light in the night.
I have discovered the secret of Voynich.
A policeman waved me off,
I who have spent the last few years begging.

The moon has a carnivorous smile,
The ghosts of the cryptographers Jesuits
Invade the dark asphalt,
And my dog rests on my wrinkled thigh.

Radiocarbon dating,
The memoirs of a Prague alchemist,
The Institute of Chicago, the study of pigments,
And 170,000 glyphs separated by thin gaps.

They were not as effective as I was.
Did Queen Christine of Sweden save the manuscript?
US Navy cryptographers see multiple authors.
Did the Devil get his hands on the parchment?

It is a fist of light in the night.
I have discovered the secret of Voynich.
My secret flies away and attaches itself to the wings of birds.
Who will believe a beggar who smells like wine?

It was January; a Yale student
Dropped a copy of the parchment near my boxes.
I spent five years deciphering the herbarium.
I studied every image, every gilt.

The soldier with the crossbow on a page smiled at me.
The pansies, violets and ferns,
The constellations of the Zodiac
Scintillated on the illuminated pages.

Silence has invaded the dirty city now.
The rain bears the horizon with its liquid arms.
I looked for Voynich's smile in the folds of the twilight.
The sun had set; the white night opened its lashes.

God and I

The sky is torn open, a spectral liquid emanates from it.
My sandals raise the dust of the bombs.
My legs hurt; I have trampled the night, the ages.
The wind brought me the news of the graves.

A church rises up, like a brass knuckle.
The faithful are flies attracted by the sky.
The door is wide open; the wind roars in vain.
The red clouds vomit an avalanche of bile.

He entered without a sound; he stands prostrate
Near the altar and his head rests in his dirty hands.
The mute Devil listens to the organ begging him.
He enjoys every empty chair, every sepulchral silence.

The faithful have left God to join the banks
Of a tormented river, and bathe in a Time
Deserted by angels, in which the candles blacken.
The sun can't help it, for it only burns for a moment.

The sky is stale; a profane perfume emanates from it.
My sandals have walked on the concrete of the great capitals.
I have caressed the cheeks of believers and wisemen,
But where was God, where was his son? The nave moans.

White agony, seconds spent eye to eye
With an angel fallen in dust, passion of a bitter Christ.
Books scratched with the sweat of History—this infernal God
Who blows in the churches and put out the lights.

To Auson

Nouvelle Aquitaine, a crystal sky,
The tender green of amaranths,
A poet who loves Greek stories
Marries the daughter of the consul,

And in an estate near Bordeaux
Their flowery graves
Collect the fallen pinecones.
The ashes of time invite itself here.

And the wind blows on the manor
In Auson near the Atlantic.
The petals of fate
Have inscribed your names in the granite.

Lovers of a day, 1,700 years have erased
Your smiles during the banquet
And the discreet glance of the poet
Towards a damsel, in secret.

Rhetorician, a young Alaman slave,
Served you as an inkwell at nightfall.
She copied your manuscripts,
And you read History to her.

1,700 years have passed
Since Auson took the pen
To transcribe your disheveled days.
Your graves blacken the land of Aquitaine.

And the wind blows on the manor
In Auson near the Atlantic.
A vineyard took the taste of soil
Of your flowery romances.

History's withered roses

A crate of weapons hidden under the moon
Don't forget me, I will win the war, wait for me.
The explosives have been buried under the sand,
The fields sparkle, the night takes me in its bosom,
A singer rains patriotic notes
Don't forget me, I'll win the war for you,
But the railway shakes, the wagons are loaded
With forgotten grenades, and the moon is a white sun.
My blue shirt is soaked with sweat, are you thinking of me?
We hear shots fired through the mist,
The whistle of a rifle under the stars, the voice of a friend,
Wait for me. I will win the war for you.
And if death's talons close on my chest,
Wait till the rain hides thee from enemy's eyes
To come and bloom my grave with wilted roses
And if I can't win the war,
Know that I have twisted the neck of History so that you love me
In the silent night, in the muffled whispers,
I married the blue night of your memory
And if I don't win the war
Because others than me have won it,
Wait for the rain to hide you from enemy eyes
And bent over the grass that covers my grave,
Think that the war cannot be won by angels,
And go away from my grave

www.ingramcontent.com/pod-product-compliance
Lightning Source LLC
Chambersburg PA
CBHW071138090426
42736CB00012B/2157